What I Like About Me

All rights reserved. No part of this publication may be reproduced, stored in a retrieval system, or transmitted in any way by any means electronic, mechanical, photocopy, recorded or otherwise without the prior permission of the copyright holder, except by reviewer who may quote brief passages in a review to be printed in magazine, newspaper or radio/TV announcement, as provided by USA copyright law. The author and the publisher will not be held responsible for errors within the manuscript.

Copyright 2025
ISBN 979-8-9991700-4-0

Printed in the USA

Photography
Thru My Eyes Photography
By K. Akins

This book is dedicated to all the families and children who have participated in the Morgan Ministries Outreach Mentoring Program. Your journey, growth, and resilience continue to inspire us every day.

A special tribute is given to **Dametrion Evans,** whose laughter, energy, and spirit brought joy to everyone around him. Though he is no longer with us, his memory remains forever in our hearts.

While this book is a collection of cherished moments—capturing two summers filled with fun, games, and activities—what stands out most is the way these children have embraced their self-worth. Watching them learn to love themselves and celebrate *"What I Like About Me"* truly inspiring.

None of this would have been possible without the unwavering support of my husband, Jay, and our dedicated volunteers and teachers.

We are especially grateful for the incredible partnership and support from Ability Housing's staff and management, the Orange County Sheriff's Office, and the City of Orlando (Mercy Drive Kidz Zone). Your commitment has been an anchor of strength, making a lasting impact on our mission.

With gratitude,
Elizabeth Morgan
Morgan Ministries, Inc.

At the heart of every community lies its future—the children who grow, learn, and aspire to become the leaders of tomorrow. The Mercy Drive Kidz Zone is more than just a place; it's a beacon of hope, a safe haven, and a launchpad for dreams.

Our mission is rooted in a profound belief in the potential of every child. We are committed to fostering an environment that nurtures growth, builds resilience, and empowers young minds to achieve greatness. Serving the Mercy Drive community is not just a responsibility; it is a privilege. We are inspired daily by the energy, creativity, and determination of the children and families who call this area home.

Through collaboration, compassion, and unwavering dedication, we aim to address the challenges that underserved communities often face. But beyond addressing needs, we strive to create opportunities—opportunities for education, exploration, and self-discovery. We believe that when a community comes together to invest in its youth, it sets the foundation for a brighter, more equitable future.

Thank you to everyone who supports the Mercy Drive Kidz Zone and shares in our vision of empowering our community. Together, we are planting the seeds for a stronger, more vibrant tomorrow.

In service and solidarity,
Oneka Burnett and the Mercy Drive Kidz Zone Team

At Ability Housing, we wholeheartedly embrace the belief that "it takes a village to raise a child." This guiding principle shapes our mission to cultivate vibrant, supportive communities where every individual—especially our youth—has the opportunity to flourish.

We are privileged to collaborate with Liz Morgan of Morgan Ministries, whose steadfast dedication to the youth at Village on Mercy beautifully embodies the spirit of collective care. Liz's unwavering strength, determination, and faith-driven leadership have made her an indispensable partner to our organization. Her passion for nurturing the youngest members of our community ensures that their voices are heard, their needs are prioritized, and they are welcomed with open arms and without judgment.

Through Morgan Ministries, Liz offers vital programs such as after-school tutoring and summer camps, focusing on life enrichment, financial literacy, self-esteem, and academic support. These initiatives provide children with a safe and encouraging environment where they can grow, learn, and reach their fullest potential. Liz Morgan's remarkable contributions have profoundly enriched the lives of our residents, exemplifying the true power of community partnership. Her work is a testament to the positive change that is possible when we unite around a shared vision.

Indeed, it truly does take a village—and together, we are building a brighter future for all.

In gratitude,

Ability Housing

A Review

I found this book to be tightly centered and brief, but a rich compilation of very specialized thoughts/themes the children have devised as they look at themselves, their perceptions of themselves, and the parts of their bodies they admire, highlight, and celebrate. These children, surrounded by those who love them, are able to focus and highlight their physical features that bring them pleasure and impetus to continue down the roads of life. These children are active creators of their own community in this interesting way.

I can sense in reading their comments a focus on the part(s) of their bodies that inspire them to learn and continue to interact socially with their friends, teachers, and those who care for them. I can see in their expressions - a seriousness that binds them towards a future that will hopefully challenge them as they evolve into the young adults they will become. I would really like to see how this journal will change or advance their journey over the next five years as they revisit the themes they have displayed here. I would further love to have them come together again in about ten years to gather additional information on how these young children have moved from the thoughts shown here to people of purpose and conviction in their future. Dare we ask how their thoughts today about themselves will foster another generation of kids from this group as they cross the thresholds of parenting those they nurture some years from now?

I am now wondering what the parents would put into print of these noble ones and how the parents might respond if an anthology were written as they (the parents) wrote about "What I Like About Me". This is the first time I have given serious thoughts about the title discussed and shown here (What I Like About Me).

Bishop Cliff Morris

Foreword

In a world that often tries to define who we are before we even have the chance to speak, "What I Like About Me" stands as a powerful declaration of self-love and identity. This book gives voice to African American teens as they celebrate their uniqueness, their beauty, their strength, and the vibrant heritage that shapes who they are.

Each story, reflection, and poem within these pages echoes with pride and honesty—reminding us that self-acceptance is not arrogance, but courage. These young voices are not waiting for permission to shine; they are illuminating their own paths and inspiring others to do the same.

As you read, you'll feel the rhythm of confidence, resilience, and hope. You'll hear laughter, truth, and dreams, reaching beyond limitations. This is more than a collection of words—it's a mirror for every young person learning to love themselves in full color.

May this book remind every reader that what makes us different is what makes us extraordinary.

John Ellis

Board Chair
Morgan Ministries

Morgan Ministries

Jay and Elizabeth founded Morgan Ministries in 1996. The Morgans are a "Power Couple" making a positive impact on the lives of men, women, and children in Central Florida.

This ministry has touched the lives of thousands in Central Florida through its compassionate outreach programs focused on youth mentoring, feeding and serving the homeless, and transitional home for women. The message is spread within the community through a weekly radio broadcast and social media channels.

The Morgans are dedicated to empowering individuals to be productive leaders who will pass on the legacy of self-worth and purposeful citizenship.

MINISTRY FOCUS

Radio Program   Community Outreach
Homeless Feeding   Mentoring

Currently, Evangelist Morgan leads a weekly Prayer Line to provide guidance, inspiration, and support to women facing various circumstances that require assistance.

In memory of

Da'Metrion White

Aamiyah

I like my hair.

It's beautiful and my hair will grow in into the braids.

I like my hair because it's long.

I like my hair because it has colors

I like my hair because other people like my hair because it's long.

I like to put it in a ponytail,

and sometimes it gets in my face,

and it blows in the wind.

A'Liviah

I love my eyes because I can see.
I can see my mommy and can look in the mirror at myself.
And when I look at myself, I see how pretty I am.

I can look and see what I am writing.
I can read books with my eyes too.

My eyes are very important to me.
I do not want to lose them.
I will be lost without them.

Alianna Petty

I like my face because it's soft and beautiful and strong.

I do facials because it helps my skin stay nice and soft.

I have beautiful eyelashes.

I love the way my nose is perfect and fits my face.

My ears are tiny and cute, and they fit my face.

I have a dimple on one side, and it makes me unique.

I love my eyebrows.

Finally, I love my long beautiful soft hair and edges.

I love my face.

Amier

My skin color – I think I got pretty skin.

I like the color of my skin.

It's not dark brown or light brown,

It's a nice brown.

I like my skin because its soft.

I like my skin because sometimes I can scratch it.

I just like my skin because it's my skin.

Amore

My name is Amore
and I love my eyes. They help me to see my mom and dad.
I love the shape of my eyes and the color of my eyes.
I can see movies with my eyes and all the people I love.
I can do things with my eyes; I can move them up and down.
I can see how to play my game.
I can see "Sammy" the dog.
I can see where I'm walking with my eyes.
I can see colors with my eyes.
I love my eyes

Anibella

I love my hands because I can grow my nails long.
I love my hands because my mom can paint my nails different colors.
I love for my nails to be painted pink – that's my favorite color.

I love my hands because I can pick up things.
I can put my clothes on with my hands.

I can play my favorite games with my hands.
I can write and draw because I have hands.
I can feel how soft things are with my hands.
I love my hands.

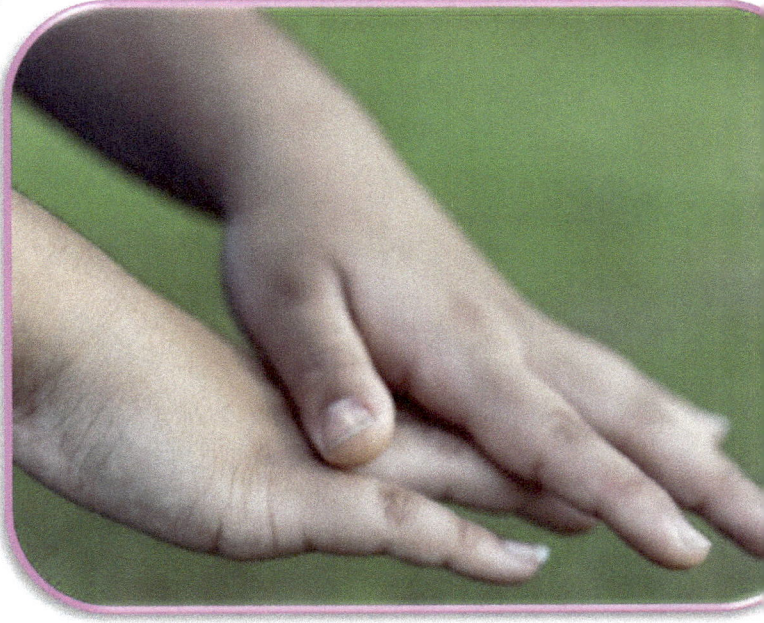

A'Niylah

I like my teeth because I get to brush them and keep them clean!

I love my teeth because I get to go to the dentist's office.

When I get there, I have to wait, but it's ok!

The dentist office let us play with their toys!

But there is one sad thing.

Since the virus, the dentist office can't let us play with their toys anymore.

We can't play with the toys anymore, so I just watch TV!

When they call me, I'm so scared!

But with my mom by my side, I calm down and I feel much better.

When they finish cleaning, my teeth are sparkling!

Afterwards, I get to choose a toothbrush and we can choose any color we want!

So don't be scared to go to the dentist…it's really fun!

Braniya

The best part of me is my eyes because…
I can see!
I can blink!
I can see people.
I can play games.
And I can look at people when they are talking!

My eyes help me see my schoolwork.

My eyes help me to see to help others.

The best part of me is my eyes.

They are my Chinese eyes!

It's because of my eyes how I got my nick name, Chyna.

I'm happy I have them to see, because my uncle is blind and can't see.

It is so sad.

Camryn

I love my brain because all I know in life
and can remember is because of my brain.
I do good in school because of my brain
The knowledge I have and what and how I think is because of my brain.
I could not run or play or move without my brain working properly.
My brain lets me know if danger is near.
My brain lets me know when I'm tired and when to go to bed.
My brain lets me know if something is too hot or too cold.
Without my brain I could do nothing.
I love my brain!

Damisa

What I love about myself are my eyes.

I like the color, the shape and size of my eyes.

With my eyes I can see my mom and dad.

I can see how to do things with my eyes.

If I did not have eyes I would not be able to see anything.

I can see where to walk with my eyes.

I can see nature, like green grass, flowers, trees and animals.

I can see colors with my eyes.

I can see how to step up and down with my eyes.

With my eyes I can see my favorite animals like dogs and cats.

I really like my eyes.

David

The best part of me is my legs!
I can run with them, and I can walk with them!
I can kick stuff and make them move.
And I like my feet because I can bounce!

I like my arms because I can hug my mom and dad.
And I can hug my grandma!
My arms hold my hands, so they won't fall off!
I like my hands!
I can feel and touch things
I can open things and close things.
I can put my socks on, and I can put on my shoes!

I like my neck too.
I can move my neck and it won't crack!

But I really do like my legs.
I can rest them and
make them stronger!
They can grow!

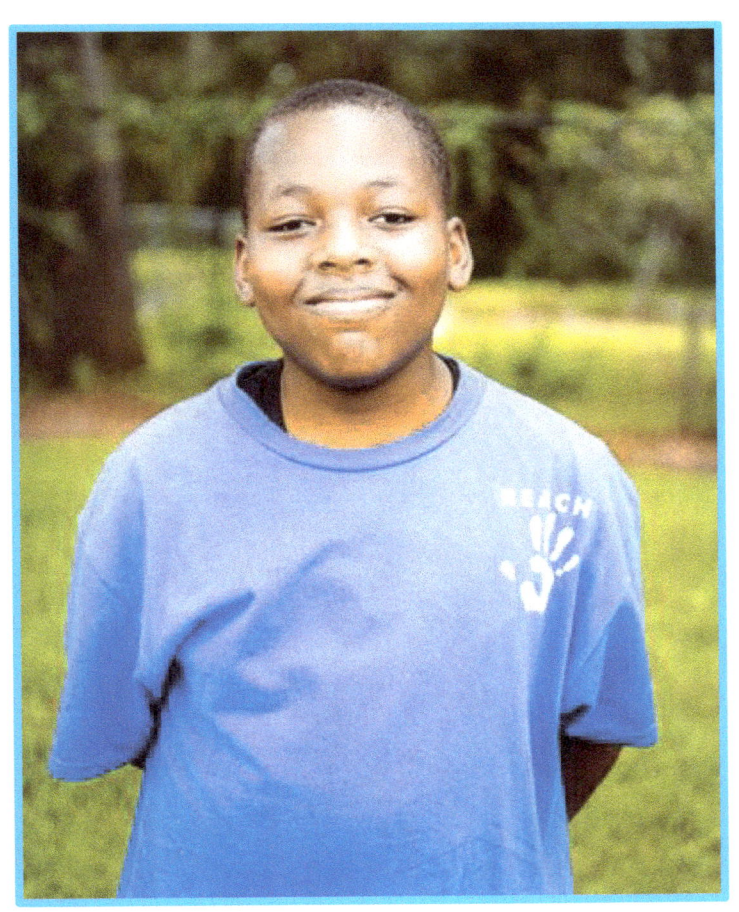

Elijah

I like my eyes because I can SEE
I like my eyes because I can SEE
a ball,
and a football,
and a soccer ball,
and a dog,
and a tiger.

I can SEE the pool,
I can SEE my mom, my dad and my grandma!

I can SEE a rainbow!
I can SEE the sun.
I can SEE the sky.
I can SEE PS5.

Hazel

I like my hair because my hair is curly, long and beautiful.
My hair reminds me of a black bear because my hair is black!
But it looks brown when it is touched by the sun.

When my hair is wet, it becomes straight.
I really like to wear my hair in braids.
It makes me feel happy!
But most of all my hair is the best part that
describes me… my HAZEL HAIR!

Jakari

The best part of me is my hands.

I can catch a football.

I can grab a water bottle.

I can scratch my legs.

I can take out the trash.

I can grab a broom.

I can read a book.

I can comb my hair.

I can play games on my PS8 and PS5.

I can eat my food.

I can draw a picture.

I can hug people and shake their hands.

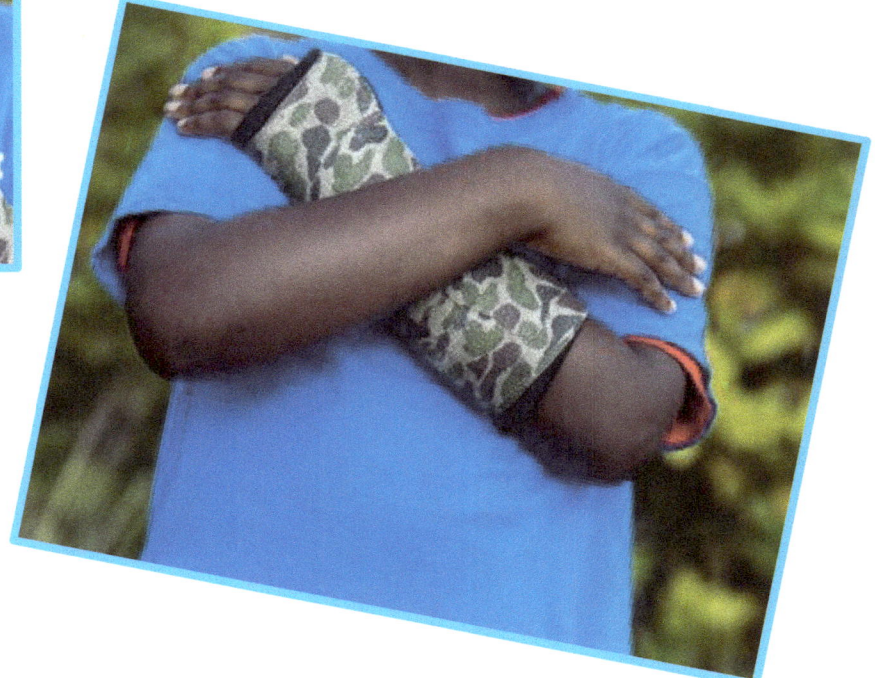

JaMarcus

I like my legs!

I like it because I can run fast playing football.

And if someone is chasing me, I can run even faster!

I like my legs! They can do cool dances!

I like my legs because if I had no legs, I would not be able to play football nor dance.

That's why I like my legs!

And my legs help me to jump high!!

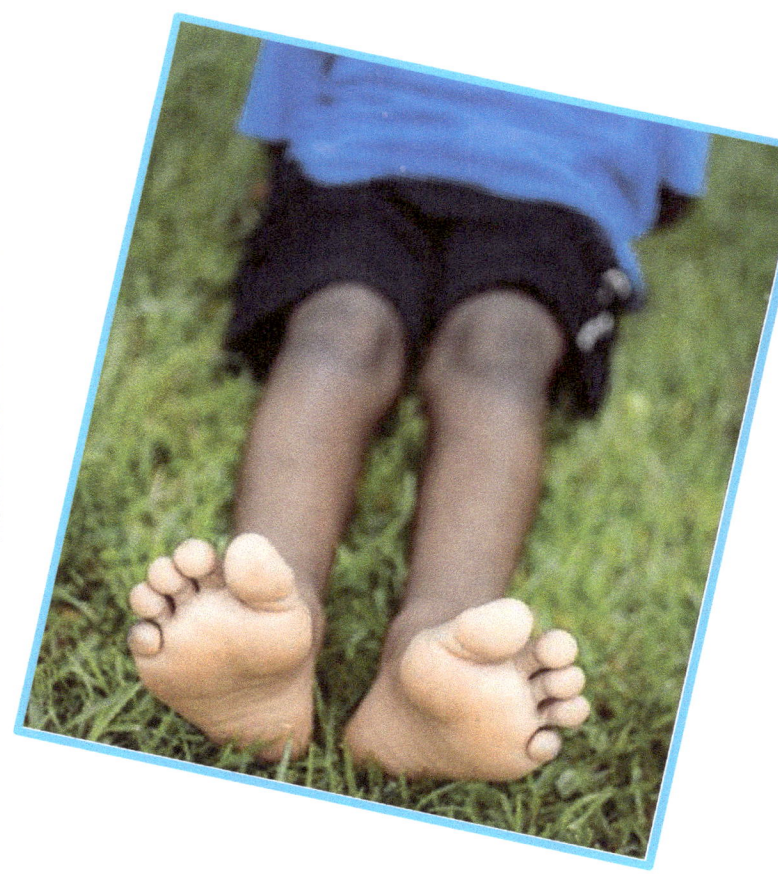

Ja2uevious

I love a lot of things about myself

But the thing I love the most is my legs.

I love to run and walk, and they help me move around.

I can kick and do different tricks with my legs.

They also help me run to fast.

I can fight with my legs

And my legs help me to chase my dog when she runs away.

I love my legs.

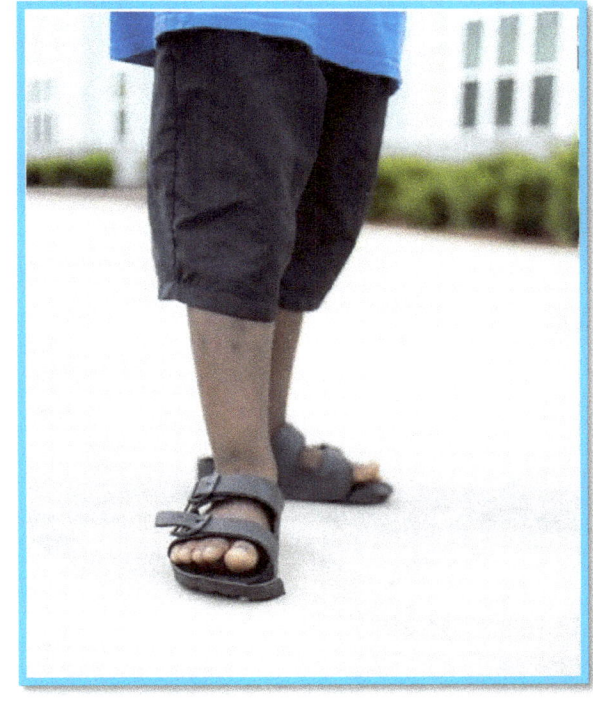

Ladinah

I love my eyes – how pretty they look.

I can see with my eyes.

I like the color of my eyes.

I like to look at the blue sky and the clouds.

I can blink really fast with my eyes.

I can see how to touch things with my eyes.

I like to wash my eyes in the morning when I wake up and at night before I go to sleep.

My eyes are very important to me and I'm glad that I have them attached to my body.

Miracle

The best part of me is my hair.

I love my hair!

My hair is fun!

I can braid it and I can make it curly!

When my hair is wet, it becomes curly.

But when I put a hot comb in it,

My hair becomes straight!

National

I like my legs because I can run.

I can run far.

And I can run very fast!

I can walk from place to place.

I use them to walk from school.

I can use my legs to jump.

And I can jump off things too!

I want to go to Aquatica

So that I can use my legs to swim.

It will make me happy.

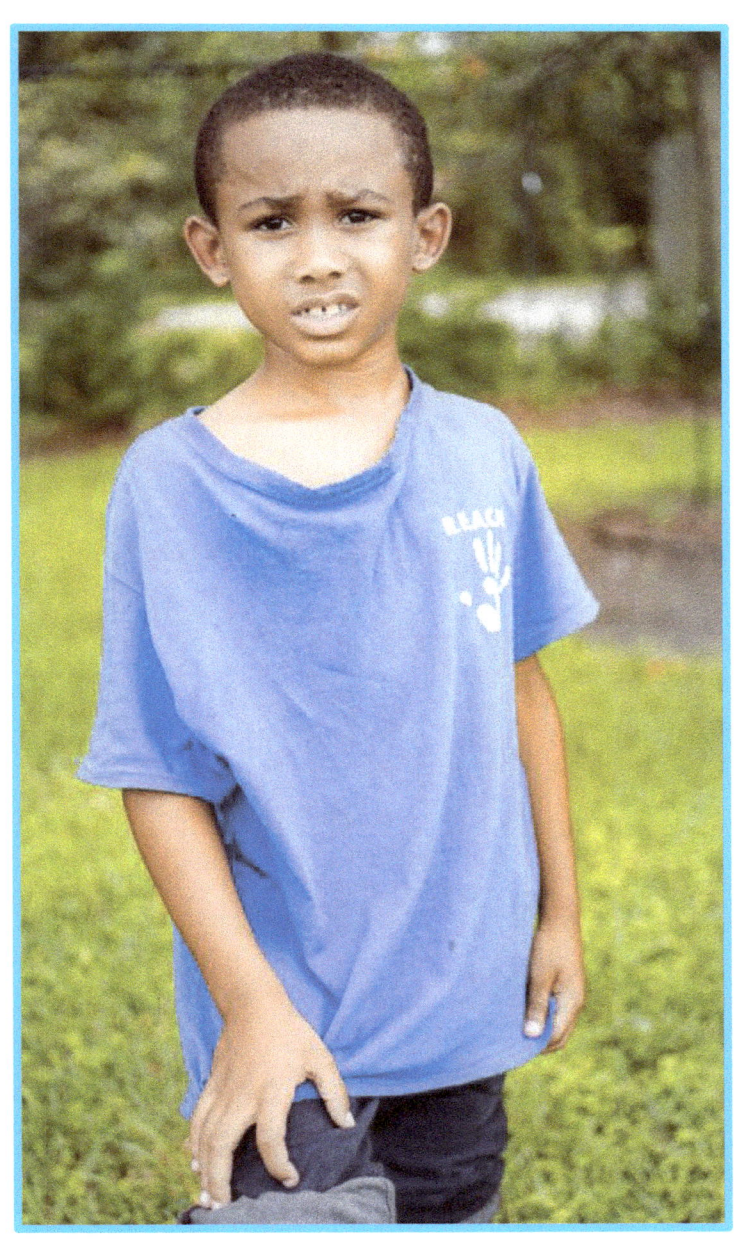

Quincy

What I love about myself is my eyes

Because my eyes are brown.

When I hear a sound

I like to see my eyes turn brighter.

I like that I can watch my favorite YouTube show with my eyes.

I like that I can express myself with my eyes.

With my eyes I can play games

And I can play football which is my favorite sport.

One day I hope to see myself on TV playing professional football.

Sandrisha

I like my hair because
every time I do my hair, people tell me how they love it!
They love my natural hair because it is brown and soft!
When they touch my hair, it feels like cloud nine!
This is the best part of me...MY HAIR!
When I was little I heard people around me say that I can be a model!
They would tell me how my brown hair matches m y dark brown skin
and my beautiful dark brown eyes.
I think I like everything about me
because everything about me matches together!
I am BEAUTIFUL!
I am DARK BROWN QUEEN
with a NATURAL brown afro and dark and lovely skin.

Sidney

I love my hands because we use our hands for a lot of things

Like picking up things.

I like that I can eat with them.

I can also play my game and ride my bike.

I can do my homework and I can hold my cousin.

I can even hold my mom's hand.

We use them for so many things in our everyday life.

I wouldn't know what to do without them.

Tahlia

I love my face because it's pretty.

I love the color of my face.

It's smooth and creamy looking.

I love my face because it shows how I feel.

I like looking at myself in the mirror

Because God made my beautiful face.

Tatyana

If I did not have a mouth,
I would not be able to talk or eat.
If I did not have my mouth,
I would not be able to breathe.

I would not be able to eat apples, chicken and so much more.
The mouth is the only place on my body where I can eat and talk!
Without my mouth, I can't enjoy a lollipop,
Talk about planes and say things to my friends!
We all need a mouth.
We need our mouths to share and play games.
Without our mouths
It would be very sad
Because I would not be able to hear my friends speak to me.